The HOME Team
Pittsburgh Penguins®

Written by Holly Preston

Illustrated by James Hearne

Always Books Ltd.

AFANFORLIFE.COM

MIX
Paper from
responsible sources
FSC® C016245
www.fsc.org

For all young PENGUINS® fans
who know there's no team like ours!

Skating with your friends is fun ...

... and so is watching the PITTSBURGH PENGUINS play.

We love to play hockey, too. Liam plays forward. Ethan plays defense. Jacob is in goal. The boys all want to play for the PENGUINS one day.

Even after playing all day, Liam dreamed only about hockey.

The only problem was Liam never scored. Ever.
The puck went high. The puck went low.
The puck went everywhere but where it was supposed to go.

How can I ever play for the PENGUINS? Liam wondered.
His sister Grace was the best goal scorer in the neighborhood.

"The PENGUINS were little boys once, too, Liam," his dad said.
"They didn't become hockey stars overnight."

His mom said, "You can learn a lot by watching what the PENGUINS do."
She'd been a PENGUINS fan forever.

The PENGUINS are great skaters.

They make big plays.

They shoot. They score!

And make a million saves.

"The only way to get better is to practice," said Jacob.
And so they practiced hard. And then came the best suprise they'd ever had.
"We're going to a PENGUINS game!" Ethan yelled.

But at the game, the PENGUINS' top scorer wasn't scoring at all!
"Something is wrong," said Liam.

The next day on the way to the rink, Liam found a shiny chain.
He put it on and ... he got a goal! And then another one!
"That's a good luck charm, for sure," Grace said.

"Our player lost his good luck charm, kids," said Dad. "Maybe *that's* why he hasn't been scoring." The children knew hockey players are superstitious. They also knew where that charm was …

... and what they had to do next!

Liam seized the moment.
"What does it take to play for the PITTSBURGH PENGUINS?" he asked.

Play like a team ...

... and with heart.

Never give up.

Believe in yourself.

"The PENGUINS are the greatest team in the NHL," said Jacob.
"We're going to be PENGUINS fans forever," added Ethan.

Everything was the way it should be.

All the next week Liam practiced and practiced.
He no longer had the good luck charm, but he had something else —
he believed in himself.

And that was all he really needed.

But Liam, like all hockey players, knew a little luck always helps ...

... especially when you're playing for the Stanley Cup®!

ABOUT THE AUTHOR

Holly Preston

Holly grew up watching NHL hockey with her brother and father. Now she creates children's picture books for professional sports teams. She hopes Penguins fans will enjoy having a book that celebrates their home team and encourages young fans to find a love of reading.

ABOUT THE ILLUSTRATOR

James Hearne

Born in London, England, James began his art career at the tender age of eight, selling drawings to guests at his grandparents' hotel. He continues to sell his whimsical illustrations around the globe as a full-time illustrator and full-time hockey fan.